SPECTACULAR SPIDERS

▼

BY LINDA GLASER

illustrated by Gay W. Holland

M MILLBROOK PRESS
Minneapolis

To Mur,
who has always given me her full encouragement
and support. Thank you.
L.G.

To Laura,
my princess, for taking my hand and leading me back
to the magic and wonder of childhood.
G.W.H.

The author and illustrator wish to thank Larry Weber,
a spectacular spider consultant.

Text copyright © 1998 Linda Glaser
Illustrations copyright © 1998 Gay W. Holland

Millbrook Press
A division of Lerner Publishing Group, Inc.
241 First Avenue North
Minneapolis, Minnesota 55401 USA

For reading levels and more information, look up this title at www.lernerbooks.com.

Library of Congress Cataloging-in-Publication Data

Glaser, Linda.
    Spectacular spiders / by Linda Glaser; illustrated by Gay W. Holland.
        p.   cm.
        Summary: Describes, in simple text and illustrations, the physical characteristics, habits, and natural environment of the garden spider.
    ISBN 978-0-7613-0353-4 (lib. bdg. : alk. paper)
    ISBN 978-0-7613-8446-5 (EB pdf)
    1. Black and yellow garden spider—Juvenile literature. [1. Black and yellow garden spider. 2. Spiders.]
I. Holland, Gay, ill. II. Title.
QL458.42.A7G58 1998
595.4'4—dc21 97-47095

⌐ctured in the United States of America
- BP – 10/1/15

Outside I have a little friend who does
spectacular things with thread.

The morning dew has left strings of sparkles
on the threads of garden spider's web.

And here is my friend—in the middle of the web—waiting for an insect to fly onto the threads.

Spider has eight skinny legs with very fine hairs that can feel when a fly is whizzing through the air.

Garden spider waits.
Very still.
Very still.
Until…

that fly gets stuck on the sticky web.

Then spider gets busy! And wraps a meal in thread.

Spider's legs move like fingers. They curve and turn and bend.
And spider uses those skillful legs to wrap and weave and spin.

Spider's legs are skinny and quick.
Spider can scoot and scurry and dart and dash
or scuttle away and zip like a flash.

And spider always leaves behind
a trail of dragline thread
to easily find the way back to the web.

Spider can drop out of danger and hang midair,
on a thread so thin it looks like nothing's there.

But where there's a spider there's always silk thread.

The thread grows longer and longer as spider goes

d
o
w
n

d
o
w
n

d
o
w
n

And it gets shorter
and shorter as spider
climbs

up

up

up

up

Until the thread is gone—
because spider eats it up.

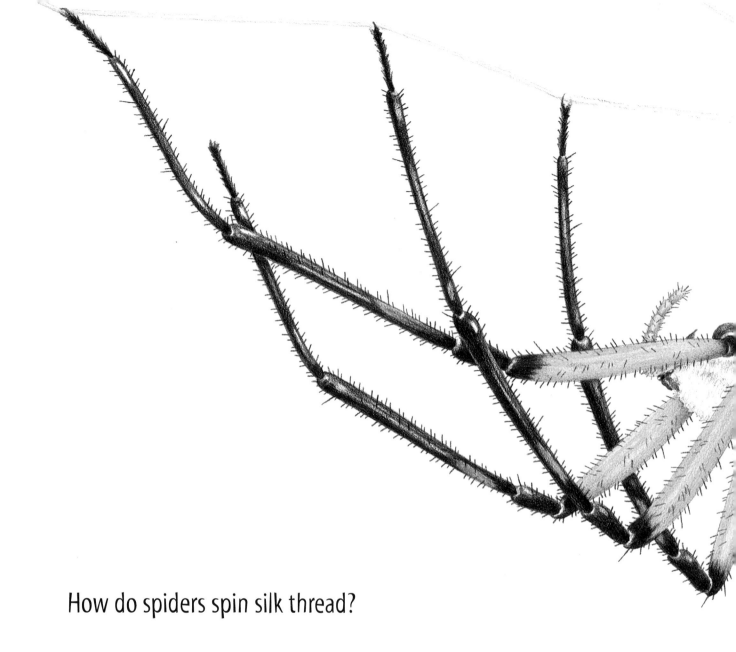

How do spiders spin silk thread?

Spiders have a place inside where liquid silk is made.

They pull the liquid out through holes
on their back ends.

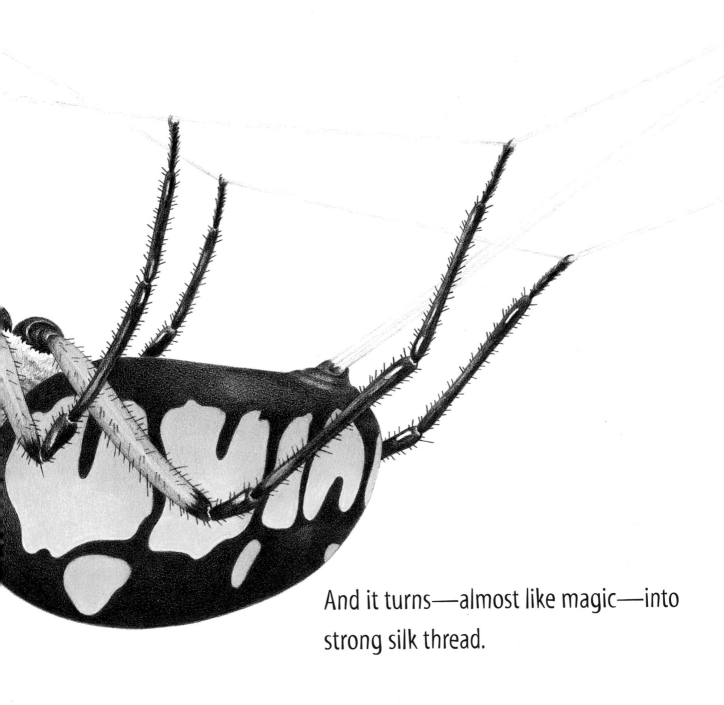

And it turns—almost like magic—into strong silk thread.

Long and stretchy. Thin and shiny. Almost see-through spider thread.

After sunset, garden spider
sends out a long silk thread
that lands on a twig and
makes a thin silk bridge.

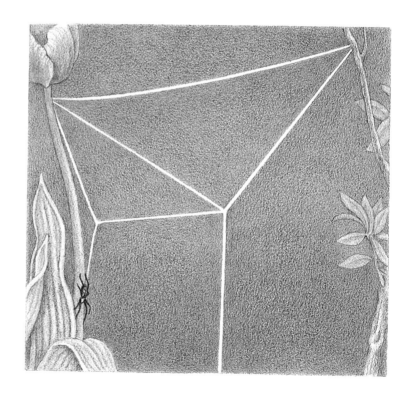

Then spider weaves the skinny spokes and sticky spirals,
until it's built a whole new web.

Spiders do all sorts of things with thread.
The mothers even use silk thread to bundle
spider eggs.

And when the baby spiderlings hatch,
they send out skinny traveling threads
that catch the wind and carry them off
to start a new life somewhere else.

Spiders are my little friends.
Spectacular spinners and weavers,
trappers and travelers.
Quietly catching insects all over the earth.

FACTS ABOUT SPIDERS

Are spiders insects?

No. Spiders are arachnids. They are very different from insects.

Insects have six legs. Spiders have eight legs. An insect's body has three main parts. A spider's body has two main parts.

A baby insect looks very different from the adult it will become. It grows bigger by molting—shedding its old "skin". And it also changes by metamorphosis into a very different-looking adult.

A baby spider looks like a tiny adult spider. It grows bigger by molting. But it always looks like a spider.

How many different types of spiders are there?

More than 35,000 types of spiders are known and identified.

Scientists believe there may be more than 35,000 other types of spiders that haven't yet been identified.

What is the name of the spider in this book?

It's a black and yellow *Argiope aurantia*, which is a common type of garden spider. Garden spiders build orb webs that can be 3 feet (90 cm) across!

The *Argiope's* web usually has a zigzag pattern in the middle.

What are some other types of spiders?

There are too many types of spiders to list them all. Here are a few spiders and the spectacular things they do:

Bolas spiders use a sticky silk ball attached to a silk thread that they toss at prey.

Crab spiders are brightly colored, often yellow or pink, to match the yellow center or pink petals of flowers where they wait for prey.

Dwarf spiders are so tiny that four or five would fit on your baby fingernail.

Fishing spiders run across water and reach below the surface to catch prey.

House spiders live in houses and quietly build webs that trap insects that come into houses.

Net casting spiders hang upside-down with a silk net to catch their prey.

Nursery web spiders wrap "gifts" and make tents. The fathers bring silk-wrapped fly "gifts" for the mothers. The mothers make silk tents to protect their babies.

Spitting spiders spit gum to stick their prey down on the ground.

Tarantulas are the biggest spiders. Their leg span can be as much as 10 inches (25.5 cm). The female keeps her egg sac in a burrow and guards it for seven weeks.

Trap-door spiders live underground in a silk lined tunnel. They make a trapdoor of silk and dirt with a silk hinge. Then they open the silk door slightly and wait for prey to pass by.

Water spiders live in air bubbles underwater in ponds and streams of Great Britain and Europe.

Wolf spiders hunt for food instead of trapping food in webs. The mother carries her egg sac with her. When the spiderlings hatch, the mother carries the tiny babies on her back—piggyback style.

Zebra jumping spiders can jump 20 to 40 times their own length.

WOLF SP

Where do spiders live?

Spiders live almost everywhere on Earth except in the polar regions. Wherever insects live, there are also spiders catching and eating them. Spiders live in fields, on beaches, in forests, and in houses. There are spiders on the highest mountains, in the hottest deserts, and in the deepest valleys on Earth.

How long do spiders live?

Most spiders only live one or two seasons. Some live longer. The female bird spider, a type of tarantula, may live as long as twenty years.

Are tarantulas dangerous?

Tarantulas found in North America are shy, gentle, and harmless to people.

Are other spiders dangerous?

Spiders do a great deal of good. Very few are dangerous. Although almost all spiders have poison glands, most spiders are shy and harmless to people. Many spiders can't even break through a person's skin to bite. In the United States, the bite of a black widow or brown recluse can be harmful if not treated promptly. But deaths from spider bites are rare in North America.

Who are the spiders' enemies?

Frogs, toads, birds, fish, and praying mantises all eat spiders. Spiders eat other spiders. Some tiny flies and wasps lay eggs on a spider's body, and when the grubs hatch, they eat the spider.

People kill spiders, too. People use pesticides (poisons) to kill harmful insects, but the pesticides also kill spiders and many other creatures. This is unfortunate because spiders kill many harmful insects safely while pesticides do not.

How long have spiders lived on Earth?

Fossils show that spiders have been on Earth for 300 million years. Human beings have lived on Earth for about 2 million years. So spiders lived on Earth for millions of years before people.

How many spiders are there on Earth?

No one really knows. But once, on a piece of land the size of a football field, more than a million spiders were found! So we know that there are millions upon millions of spiders on Earth.

What types of webs do spiders build?

Different spiders build different types of webs. Garden spiders build round webs called orb webs. House spiders build tangled webs that some people call cob webs. Some spiders build funnel webs or purse webs shaped like tubes. Some build sheet webs. A few spiders even build webs shaped like triangles or rectangles.

Do all spiders make webs?

No. Only about half the known spiders make webs. For example, wolf spiders hunt for food instead of building webs to trap food. But they use silk to wrap prey, leave draglines, and wrap their eggs.

Why don't spiders get stuck in their webs?

Spiders have an oily covering on their feet to protect them from sticking. Also, spiders use sticky threads on some parts of their web and dry threads on others.

ORCHARD SPIDER

w do spiders make silk?

piders have three to seven different types
ilk glands in their bodies to make many
ds of silk—sticky, dry, thin, thick, dragline
silk to wrap victims, silk to wrap eggs.
silk comes out of the holes on their back
s. These holes are part of their silk organs
pinnerets. The silk is sent out as liquid but
an it's pulled into the air, it instantly hard-
into strong silk thread.

ll spiders make silk throughout their lives.
ne other animals make silk at certain times
heir lives, but spiders are the only animals
t make silk all their lives.

w strong is spider silk?

pider silk is the strongest known natural
er. It's stronger than any thread of the same
ckness—even steel thread of the same
ckness! Silk made by *Nephila* or golden silk
ders in the South Sea Islands is the stron-
t silk. Islanders use the yellow silk to make
ys and fish nets.

w many insects does a spider
t in one day?

One spider usually eats about one insect
ery other day. But every day, millions upon
lions of spiders around the world eat
lions upon millions of insects.

CRAB SPIDER

Why are spiders so important?

Each day, spiders kill millions upon millions of
plant-eating insects, which might otherwise eat up
plants, crops, flowers, and tree leaves. Spiders are so
plentiful all over Earth that they eat more insects
than all other insect-eating animals put together.
Although they are small, spiders do an important
job helping to keep the insect population in
balance. In this way they help protect plants, crops,
flowers, and trees all over Earth.

ABOUT THE AUTHOR AND ILLUSTRATOR

Linda Glaser is the author of many successful books for young naturalists. She holds a B.S. degree from Cornell and an M.A. in Creative Arts from San Francisco State University. A certified preschool teacher, Ms. Glaser and her husband and two children live in Duluth, Minnesota, where she teaches writing classes and does school programs. She hikes, cross-country skis, and has an organic vegetable and flower garden where she enjoys finding new spider friends.

Gay Holland holds a B.F.A. from Cal State, Long Beach, and an M.F.A. from the University of Arizona, Tucson. She has worked as an assistant professor of art at Frostburg State University in Maryland. Ms. Holland lives in Bandon, Oregon.